HOME OFFICE

Drug Education in Schools:

THE NEED FOR NEW IMPETUS

Report by the
Advisory Council
on the
Misuse of Drugs

© Crown copyright 1993
Applications for reproduction should be made to HMSO
First published 1993

ISBN 0 11 341081 6

*The Prevention
Working Group
would like to thank
all the individuals and
organisations who
assisted in the
production of
this report*

CONTENTS

List of appendices

ADVISORY COUNCIL ON THE MISUSE OF DRUGS

1

1. INTRODUCTION: WHY NEW IMPETUS IS NEEDED

Introduction

1.1 The Advisory Council on the Misuse of Drugs (ACMD) was established by the Misuse of Drugs Act 1971 with the duty to keep under review the problems of drug misuse and to advise Ministers on ways of dealing with them. This report on drug education in schools has been prepared by a Working Group of the Council, convened in 1991 to examine prevention issues, and has been endorsed by full Council. A list of membership of the Working Group including coopted members and officials is at appendix A. A definition of substances covered by the term drug education is laid out at the end of this chapter.

Background

1.2 The Working Group's initial terms of reference were: "To consider and advise, in the light of the Advisory Council's report on Prevention (published in 1984) [1] on preventive measures to reduce the risk of an individual engaging in drug misuse or to reduce the harm associated with drug misuse".

1.3 The Prevention Working Group therefore has a remit to look at all aspects of drug prevention work in the UK. The field of prevention is so large however that the Group decided it would be impractical to aim towards producing another sizeable report especially as it felt the principles outlined in its 1984 report were largely still valid. Instead, it decided it would consider specific topics in more detail.

1.4 School-based drug education was considered within the 1984 Report but there are several cogent reasons for believing that policies for strengthening the preventive response to drug use now need further consideration. These reasons, outlined below, prompted ACMD to re-establish the Prevention Working Group. The Group has taken as a priority the preparation of the present report which examines the contribution that drug education in schools can now be expected to make to strengthen overall prevention policies. Our reasons for believing that this initiative is timely are as follows:

The need for a strong overall prevention response to a worsening drug situation

1.5 The prime reason for believing it is necessary in 1992 to return to the topic of prevention is the fact that, compared with eight years ago, the drug situation in this country appears to have deteriorated. Prevalence figures are difficult to establish (we return to the question of prevalence in chapter 2), but it is worth noting that, in 1984, notifications of drug addicts to the Home Office Index were 7,410, but had risen to almost 21,000 in 1991 [2]. In 1984 AIDS and HIV were not an issue, but today, with the connection between injected drug misuse and transmission of HIV infection, the prevention of drug misuse is even more urgent. Added to this is the possibility of risky sexual behaviour whilst intoxicated by drugs and the risks of infection faced by those who resort to prostitution to finance their drug addiction. A further worrying feature is that drug misuse appears to be progressively affecting a younger population. New drugs have been added to the total range of illicit drugs available and new youth drug cultures are emerging. Recently MDMA (Ecstasy) and related drugs, along with LSD and amphetamines, have become popular with young people, especially in connection with the club/rave scene. The so-called "recreational" use of such drugs can lead to a dangerous acceptance of illegal and harmful drug use as part of everyday life. Recent deaths among young people using ecstasy are cause for particular concern. Increasingly there is an acceptance amongst some participants in sports and certain leisure pursuits of the misuse of drugs such as anabolic steroids and related substances which they believe will enhance their performance. Using such drugs is not only cheating, it is also harmful to health and encourages young people to believe that drug-taking is an acceptable part of sport. Furthermore, volatile substance abuse (aerosols, glue, solvents etc which can be misused by inhaling) causes an alarming number of fatalities. Statistics show a rising number of deaths, reaching 149 in 1990, over an age range that starts as young as nine years.

The need for strengthening school-based education

1.6 Prevention is always better than cure, but a deteriorating drug situation must give urgency to a review of what policies can be put in place to strengthen prevention. The Working Group believes that a strengthening of school-based education is feasible and urgently needed and we have therefore taken this topic as a priority starting point for a reexamination of drug prevention.

1.7   The efficacy of drug education in schools is by its nature difficult to assess scientifically.   Education will interact with many other contextual factors and its unique influence cannot easily be parcelled out within a research design.   Short-term classroom experiments are easy to conduct but controlled designs to assess broad educative programmes in the long term are costly and difficult.   What such education is hoping to achieve is, however, not just short-term gains but medium and long-term benefits in individual capacity to make informed and healthy choices as a young person makes his or her way through life.   Easily measurable short-term change in attitudes in a classroom questionnaire cannot measure that individual's actual change in behaviour or in coping skills.   However, recent research suggests that school-based drug education which starts early in a child's school career, which is delivered with optimum persistence and intensity and which uses multiple techniques and seeks actively to involve pupils, has good evidence to support its impact.   This is the positive perspective in which this report will frame its recommendations. (We return to this issue in chapter 3 and successive chapters.)

The need to reconsider drug education within a changing school system

1.8 With the introduction of the National Curriculum in England and Wales, the changes which are under way as a result of increasing the number of grant maintained schools ("opted-out" schools), the new arrangements for financing schools and the new systems for inspecting schools, the organisational basis through which drug education is likely to be delivered has changed significantly since 1984 and that in itself constitutes an important reason for an updating of ACMD's advice.

1.9   The Government's recent white paper on education in England and Wales: "Choice and Diversity: A new framework for schools" [3] stresses the importance of a strong moral dimension and how the general atmosphere and ethos of a school is also an important factor in a good education.   An effective preventive health programme which includes a well-planned, consistent drug education element plays an important role in supporting such an ethos.

1.10 The importance of preventive health was outlined in another recent Government white paper: "The Health of the Nation: A strategy for health in England" [4]. This white paper included a section on "healthy schools", stating the government's commitment to participating in an initiative on healthy schools being developed by the World Health Organisation, the European Community and the Council of Europe and to setting up in England with the assistance of the Health Education Authority "a pilot network of health promoting schools which will develop and assess the effectiveness of strategies for changing and shaping pupils' patterns of behaviour, with the aim of safeguarding their long-term good health" (page 27). Drug education should play an important role in such an initiative.

1.11 Similar documents have been issued recently in Wales (Plan for Action 3: The Agenda for 1992-94) and Scotland (Scotland's Health: a challenge to us all" Published by HMSO, 1992)[4]. Both documents laid emphasis on the importance of preventive health in all aspects of life. The Scottish document for example stressed the importance of health education in schools, recognising that "schools are singularly important because of their role in shaping the habits and behaviour of young people".

Scope of the report

1.12 In order to produce as timely and concise a report as possible, we have confined ourselves to schools and, although the report makes mention of the school's contacts with other agencies and the question of children in care, we have not allowed ourselves to stray further into the wider issue of the community as a whole, which is a major subject which we felt to be beyond the scope of this report.

1.13 The report starts by examining the scale of the problem and the role that schools can play in drug prevention. It then describes the present situation and suggests how schools themselves might organise their programme of drug education. It includes the role of parents and outside agencies such as police liaison officers, and examines the provision of training for teachers. Finally the report summarises key points and makes recommendations for the future.

Definitions and substances covered:

1.14   In this report we use the term "education about drugs" to refer to education about illegal drugs, misuse of medicinal products, and volatile substances (that is gases such as butane and products containing solvents such as glue, which can be misused by inhaling). We have not discussed different drugs in detail except where it is necessary for the sake of clarity, although we recognise that volatile substances present some particular problems. We have not examined the issue of volatile substance abuse in depth because the Working Group intends to produce a separate report on this. Where a distinction needs to be made between illegal drugs, the misuse of medicinal products (whose misuse may be illegal depending on the circumstances) and volatile substances (whose abuse is not illegal), we have endeavoured to make this clear in the text. Alcohol and tobacco are outside the remit of the Advisory Council. However, much of what is written about drug education is relevant to the wider field of substance misuse including alcohol and tobacco and it is sensible for drug education to be delivered in the context of an overall substance misuse approach.

1.15   Previous Advisory Council reports have used the term "problem drug taker" (ie any person who experiences social, psychological, physical or legal problems related to use of drugs), eg in the 1982 Treatment and Rehabilitation Report [5] and "problem drug use", such as in the 1990 Training Report [6]. However, we felt that in the case of schools, the term "drug misuse" was more appropriate, given that from the point of view of parents and schools any form of drug use other than proper use of prescribed medicines is quite clearly a serious problem.

2. THE EXTENT OF THE PROBLEM

2.1   There is limited statistical and research information available on the health-related behaviour of young people.   There is clearly a need for more research into the extent and nature of drug misuse among the young and the problems associated with it.   It is not possible from the data available to make even a very rough estimate of the proportion of school age children in the UK who try drugs and different surveys will produce different results depending on the way in which the survey is carried out, the geographical area, the size of the sample, the age range, the schools and so on.   However we have examined a number of recent surveys which help to build up a picture of the extent of the problem.   We examine these roughly in chronological order, beginning with the most recent.

2.2   Preliminary findings of the first stage of a longitudinal survey of 776 14-15 year olds in the North West of England in 1991 [7] showed that 59% had been offered drugs and 36% had tried a drug: 32% cannabis, 14% "poppers" (alkyl nitrites), 13% LSD, 12% solvents (volatile substances), 10% "magic mushrooms" (psilocybin), 10% amphetamine, and 6% ecstasy (MDMA).   One in five had tried a drug in the past month.

2.3   A survey of health-related behaviour in Wales [8] by the Health Promotion Authority for Wales in 1990 included a study of 2,239 15 year olds which found that 21% had tried drugs at least once and around a tenth had used one of the drugs listed in the survey within the past month, mostly cannabis or volatile substances.   Very few reported multiple or regular drug misuse.   A much smaller scale survey [9] carried out in Mid-Glamorgan, an economically deprived area of Wales, from a sample of 13,437 school children aged between 13 and 18 years, found rather higher levels of use: 10% had used drugs in the last week of which 49% were illegal drugs (cannabis accounted for 75% of them), 27% were volatile substances and 23% were 'over the counter' medications.

2.4   A research project carried out by Strathclyde University between 1987 and 1989 [10], to evaluate the effectiveness of drug education in Scotland, included a survey of the prevalence of drug misuse among around 1,000 pupils of both sexes, aged between 12 and 16, from 20 different schools. The reliability of their replies was tested by including a fictitious drug "astrolite", which only 2 of the 1,000 pupils claimed to have tried. Of these 1,000 pupils, around 22% claimed to have tried illegal drugs at least once, but reported regular use (monthly or more frequent) was very low - only 2.3% for cannabis and even less for other drugs. The research also included a survey of teachers' views of the problem: they rated alcohol and tobacco as bigger problems and more prevalent in the community; they rated volatile substances as third in terms of the size of the problem and illegal drug misuse as fourth.

2.5 In 1989 an HEA/MORI survey [11] into the attitudes and behaviour of young people showed that among over 10,000 9 to 15 year-olds who responded to a question about exposure to drugs, 15 per cent said that they had been offered some type of drug. Solvents, which were included as drugs for the purposes of the survey, and cannabis, were the most likely, although 7% mentioned at least one class A drug (heroin, cocaine, crack, LSD or ecstasy). A higher proportion of older children claimed to have been offered drugs. In total 30% of 15 year olds claimed to have been offered drugs. Seven percent of the total sample claimed to have tried at least one of the drugs asked about. Cannabis was the most common drug reported. Among 15 year olds, 15% claimed to have tried cannabis, 4% "acid" (LSD), 3% amphetamine and 2% each mentioned ecstasy (MDMA) and tranquillisers. However, negative feelings towards drugs and drug taking were widespread, including 60% of experimenters agreeing that people who took drugs were stupid. On the other hand, 72% of experimenters thought that people should try drugs at some time compared to 34% of the total sample. The attitudes and behaviour of family and friends towards smoking, drinking and drug taking appeared to influence the young person's own attitudes and behaviour.

Conclusion

2.6 The relatively high levels of exposure to drugs and of first time or experimental misuse of drugs as opposed to frequent misuse underlines the importance of dissuading pupils from experimenting in the first place and persuading those who have experimented not to continue. Even allowing for the possibility that children who misuse drugs are more likely to be playing truant when a survey is carried out and, if present, might admit less readily to illegal drug misuse or to volatile substance abuse than to use of the more "socially acceptable" alcohol and tobacco, surveys indicate that the percentage of those who experiment with drugs is lower than those who regularly use alcohol or cigarettes. This underlines the need for drug education to be delivered in the context of the wider issue of health education including all forms of substance abuse.

2.7 Levels of first-time/experimental or regular illegal drug misuse appear to become more common among young people in their later teens, with some surveys finding that over a quarter of young adults have tried illegal drugs, mainly cannabis [12]. (In the case of volatile substances, levels of first time experimental use appear to increase earlier; from early to mid-teens onwards.) Trends of drug misuse as a whole in the UK appear to be steadily rising: in 1991 the number of drug addicts notified to the Home Office increased by 17 percent to almost 21,000, much the same rate as in the previous 3 years [2]. The proportion of notified addicts under 21 who are reported to be injecting drugs has remained at around 60% from 1988 to 1991 despite widespread publicity about HIV/AIDS. A similar upward trend in drug misuse can be inferred from the annual published statistics relating to drug seizures and drug offenders [2]. Furthermore these statistics show that an increasing proportion of offenders are aged under 21. In 1991, offenders aged under 21 were responsible for 85% of the increase in the total number of offenders. Since 1988 the number of offenders aged 10 to 16 years has increased steadily.

2.8 It follows that large numbers of people who pass through the education system go on to experience drug misuse problems and that an effective preventive strategy in schools must be an important weapon in tackling the drug misuse problem. Furthermore, even if only a relatively small percentage of schoolchildren regularly misuse drugs in the country as a whole, this can still amount to a considerable number of children. In some areas schools clearly do face considerable problems relating to drug misuse that cannot be ignored or swept aside. No school or parent can afford to be complacent or think that their child or children are not at risk. In particular, the rising toll of deaths from volatile substance abuse mainly among the young (149 in 1990) points to personal tragedy and a serious problem for the nation.

2.9 Any consideration of the extent of drug misuse problems among the young must include the harm associated with drug misuse. This includes not only the tragedy of the loss of young lives from accidents related to experimentation with volatile substances or using ecstasy at a "rave", but also the risks to the majority of young people who survive their experiences with drug misuse but who may be harming their health, including putting themselves at risk of HIV infection if they inject or indulge in unsafe sex when intoxicated. Furthermore their drug misuse may be disrupting their education and thus threatening their future career and livelihood, and they may be exposing themselves to the risks of a criminal record if they break the law.

3. EVALUATION OF DRUG EDUCATION: CAN SCHOOL-BASED PREVENTION ACTIVITY ACHIEVE POSITIVE RESULTS?

3.1 Demonstrating the effect of drug education in schools in isolation from the many other factors that influence health behaviour is extremely difficult and there is little up-to-date research in this field to help us address the question of how drug education in schools can be evaluated. The following considerations need to be taken into account:

a) *The audience:* An educational programme may produce different results in relation to the age, characteristics, experience and social background of the individual pupil.

b) *The environment:* The programme will have different results depending on the community in which the school is situated and the degree of availability of drugs in the community.

c) *The prevention strategy:* A school drug education programme will only be one of a number of factors influencing health behaviour. A programme which is supported by broader demand reduction strategies in the community may be expected to have more impact than a programme operating in isolation.

d) *Level of provision:* The extent to which a programme is effective in implementation will depend on a number of factors such as the level of training provided to the teachers delivering it, the amount of resources and curriculum time devoted to the subject, the quality of delivery and the aims and commitment of all involved in the programme.

e) *Delivery of education:* Although there is some literature on outcomes of drug education, it is unclear what educational processes (ie the ways in which the programme was carried out) led to these outcomes. We suspect that educational programmes as actually delivered do not always correspond to the programmes as actually planned. We consider that more attention should be paid to evaluation of processes, as well as outcomes.

f) ***Behaviourial outcome:*** A given educational programme may be more effective in relation to one drug or type of drug than another (volatile substances, for example, may raise educational issues that call for specific evaluation). Furthermore, it may discourage ever use, delay onset of use, decrease the quantity or frequency of use, discourage particularly harmful forms of use (eg injecting) or encourage cessation of use and/or seeking help. Any one programme may be more effective in achieving one or more of these outcomes than others.

3.2 The above points demonstrate the complexity of evaluating school drug education programmes. Any evaluation which fails to take account of all the factors involved in education will provide misleading results.

Review of Research

3.3 There are few recent British studies on how to evaluate the effectiveness of drug education in schools. There is a substantial study by Strathclyde University of some relevance [10] but it is not a longitudinal study. Consequently one has to turn elsewhere, to the United States for example. There considerable research has been done although American researchers would argue that much still remains to be tackled. It is fair to say that the relevant literature has, in the past, produced mixed results, leading to a degree of uncertainty, as reflected in the cautious approach adopted in our 1984 Prevention Report (in sections 6.9 and 6.10 and appendix F).

3.4 Some of the more recent American research suggests that drug education in schools may be contributing to a reduction in drug use (Johnson, 1991 - [13]). Surveys of drug use among high school seniors point to a reduction in the use of marijuana/cannabis and cocaine, at least from the late 1980s. Structural factors such as the end of the Vietnam war, recession, and changes in the age composition of the population may have helped to bring about this reduction in drug use, as Johnson notes. But there is also evidence that the reduction in use could in part be attributable to drug prevention efforts in schools and in the media. Those same high school seniors showed increasing awareness of the risk of harm from regular drug use, while they also gave increasingly favourable ratings to the drug education to which they were exposed.

3.5 While Johnson's findings are suggestive rather than conclusive, some recent evaluations of drug education programmes in the United States have pointed more specifically to short-term reductions in the onset of drug use, within 18 months of intervention (Hawkins et al., 1991 - [14]). Hawkins and his co-authors cite a number of recent studies which point to short-term behaviourial change, as a result of extensive drug education involving a combination of social awareness training, resistance skills and other approaches. Unfortunately, in those few studies with a follow-up period of two years or longer, initial benefits disappeared. As Hawkins et al. note, one possible conclusion is that the initial intervention should have been stronger; alternatively, while that intervention may originally have been sufficiently strong, it should later have been consolidated or reinforced more strongly. Consequently more research is needed, involving longitudinal panel studies.

3.6 Although the prevention literature review by the Institute for the Study of Drug Dependence [15] is generally sceptical about the ability of drug prevention education in schools to influence behaviour, reference is made to the value of the "life skills" approach, in the context of a chapter on resistance skills (pages 21-22). With some caveats, Dorn and Murji point to a number of evaluations of life skill programmes, additional to those mentioned above, which resulted in appreciable delays in onset of drug taking. No doubt there is still a need for caution and, as Dorn and Murji also conclude, for further research. However, the picture now beginning to emerge is an increasingly positive one.

3.7 A recent review by Dr Reginald Smart (Smart 1992 - [16]) provides a useful appraisal of current research findings in Canada. It concluded that "the best programs combine several approaches and should contain material on peer influences and refusal skills". One example of life skills training which has been used and favourably evaluated in the United States is the project which was studied by Ahlen and Merrick [17].

Health behaviour research in other fields
3.8 Despite the lack of conclusive results or consensus in current research literature on the evaluation of drug education, some useful parallels can be drawn with experience in other types of health behaviour

such as eating habits, exercise, smoking and sexual behaviour. Health behaviour research has found that it is relatively easy to change knowledge and attitudes but much more difficult to bring about sustained behaviour change. However, long-term changes can be achieved. The most persuasive support for this view comes from cigarette smoking. In 1972 about 46% of the British population smoked cigarettes and by 1992 this had been reduced to 30%. These gains were not won by one simple strategy nor by any intervention applied only in the short term. The conclusions to be drawn from the wider background of health behaviour should therefore be positive but cautious. Effecting health behaviour change through education is difficult but not impossible. It is likely to require perseverance, multiple approaches and a long-term view.

Conclusion

3.9 Evidence from research specifically on drug education produces conflicting results. However, recent research points to greater grounds for optimism than we expressed in the 1984 Prevention Report, in demonstrating the ability of preventive drug education to influence attitudes and behaviour. One can now refer to a reasonably large number of multi-faceted programmes with a strong life-skills element that have been shown to lead to a delayed onset in drug taking. Given the complexities outlined above, it is proper that there should be continuing debate and that further research should be carried out. However there is reasonable consensus that drug education is more likely to be demonstrably effective when it is sustained and intensive and more likely to have impact when it teaches decision-making and life skills rather than relying entirely on a didactic approach. This consensus is supported by the practical experience of those with whom we spoke in preparation of our report and it underlies the principles and recommendations that we make in the report.

4. THE ROLE OF DRUG EDUCATION IN SCHOOLS

4.1 As we said in the introduction to this report and in the preceding chapter, influencing the climate of opinion is a long term process of which school education can only form a part. A child spends only approximately a ninth of its time in school but the influence that school has on the development of a child can be very far-reaching. The fact that it is difficult to isolate that part from the outside world and measure its effectiveness is no reason for not addressing drug education in schools. The role of schools is not only to teach specific academic subjects but also to provide pupils with more general life skills which will equip them to handle daily life and prepare them for adulthood. Indeed Section 1 of the Education Reform Act 1988 requires that the curriculum of every maintained school in England and Wales should "promote the spiritual, moral and cultural, mental and physical development of its pupils and of society", and prepare them for the "opportunities, responsibilities and experiences of adult life". The recent White Paper on education referred to in the introduction supports this philosophy [3]. Guidance issued in December 1991 on a consultative basis to Scottish schools included a coherent and progressive set of health targets to be attained by all pupils before the end of their second year of secondary education. Drug education is an essential element of a comprehensive health education programme.

4.2 Examples of the general life skills schools teach include providing sex education, awareness of health and welfare services, information about nutrition and health, and alcohol and drug education. The National Curriculum Council (NCC)'s guidance note on health education [18] states that:

"Schools have a responsibility to provide all pupils with accurate information about health matters, to help them clarify the attitudes and values which influence health choices and to promote the acquisition of healthy patterns of behaviour. This will require the consideration of health education as part of the formal curriculum and as something which permeates the ethos of a school. This includes, for instance, the quality of relationships within a school, the example set by teachers, the physical environment and a school's facilities."

4.3   In line with the recommendations of ACMD's 1984 Prevention Report and as we discussed in preceding chapters, we believe that drug education should be part of a broader preventive health programme. This programme needs to take account of the wider community and the influences on the life of a child outside the school. The above-mentioned NCC guidance note states that:

"A school has a powerful impact on the development of healthy lifestyles but it is only one influence among many. When developing a health education policy or programme, schools will need to consider other influences such as the family, community, peer group, media, legislation and the backgrounds of pupils."

The note goes on to advise that:

"In devising a health education programme which covers the formal curriculum and the wider aspects of school life, schools may wish to seek assistance from governors, parents and members of the local community."

4.4 Drug education should be an important element of a health education programme. At a time when the education system itself is evolving and undergoing major changes, it is vital to ensure that drug education receives the attention it deserves. The role of drug education in schools should be to provide pupils with opportunities to acquire knowledge and understanding about the dangers of drug misuse and to ensure that they are equipped with the attitudes and skills they need to resist pressures to misuse drugs. This is in line with recent policy documents such as the Scottish Office's policy document 'Scotland's Health' [4] which, underlining the importance of the school's role in shaping the habits and behaviour of young people, stated that: "Pupils can be presented with information and encouraged to develop skills and attitudes which will enable them to make informed and sensible choices about their health".

4.5 As we have pointed out in chapter 2 there is a continual and growing need for children to acquire the skills to avoid the risks of substance misuse and drug education should form an important part of a school's general programme of health, personal and social and health education. Included in such a programme should be a system of pastoral care and support to enable those pupils who have misused drugs and experienced problems to come forward and seek help. There is therefore a case for outlining a set of principles for drugs education which should be regarded as a sub-set of the principles of health education.

The principles of drug education in schools

4.6 In our 1984 Prevention Report [1], we described the aim of prevention as reducing the risk of an individual engaging in drug misuse or reducing the harm associated with drug misuse. The aim and objectives set out below should be read in the general context of the overall aim of prevention as described in our 1984 report. However in the context of school drug education we felt that a more specific aim and objectives should be set out. In the list below we define the *aim* as being the overall direction and *objectives* as being the measurable goals or targets which will help us move in that direction. We discuss the points listed here in more detail in later chapters.

(a) AIM   -   The aim of drug education is to enable pupils to make healthy informed choices

(b) OBJECTIVES   (i)   *Increasing knowledge, changing attitudes and enhancing skills*

-    To provide opportunities for pupils to acquire knowledge and understanding about the dangers of drug misuse

-    To provide opportunities for pupils to be equipped with the knowledge, attitudes and skills they need to avoid the misuse of drugs and to help reduce school problems associated with drug misuse where locally appropriate

(ii)   *Behaviour*

-    To minimise the number of young people who ever engage in drug misuse

19

- To delay the age of onset of first use for those who do experiment at any time

- To minimise the proportion of users who adopt particularly dangerous forms of misuse

- To persuade those who are experimenting with or misusing drugs to stop

- To enable any pupils who are misusing drugs or who have concerns about the misuse of drugs to seek help

(iii) *Citizenship*

- To increase knowledge of social and personal issues relating to drugs in line with the National Curriculum

- To enhance young people's capacity to contribute to school policies on drug misuse and wider community matters

- To enhance young people's decision-making skills more generally, using drug education as a vehicle

- To enhance later parenting skills in relation to prevention of drug misuse when pupils reach adulthood

(c) CONTEXT - Drug education should be provided in the broader context of the teaching of health and personal and social education as part of a pupil's life skills and preparation for adulthood

- It should aim to involve parents and encourage them to take an interest

- It should be delivered in the context of the school as part of the community

- It should take account of the age, sex and cultural/social background of the pupils at which it is targeted

- It should take account of the local circumstances and culture of the community

- It should provide factual and accurate information backed up with consistent advice

- it should aim to teach pupils the necessary social and personal skills described in b.1 above

(d) CONTENT, METHODS & ORGANISATION
- It should be delivered in a clear and honest manner that informs without encouraging drug misuse

- It should encourage active pupil participation backed up with adequate teacher supervision

- It should be provided at regular intervals throughout the school career so as to maximise its effectiveness

- It should be provided by teachers and other professionals with specific training in the requirements of drug education and issues relating to drug misuse

- It should be evaluated

- It should be backed up with access to advice or help for pupils with problems or concerns.

5. THE FRAMEWORK FOR DRUG EDUCATION IN SCHOOLS

5.1 Drug education needs to be planned and coordinated at three levels:

- national

- regional/district ie local education authorities

- local ie the individual schools.

5.2 The National Level: England and Wales

5.2.1 In England and Wales, drug education forms part of the statutory order for National Curriculum Science. This requires that all maintained schools in England and Wales provide some basic education about drugs. Specifically it requires pupils:

> **aged 5-7** to be introduced to ideas about how to keep healthy and about the role of drugs as medicines

> **aged 7-11** to be introduced to the fact that while all medicines are drugs, not all drugs are medicines. They should also begin to be aware of the harmful effect on health resulting from an abuse of tobacco, alcohol and other drugs

> **aged 11-14** to extend their study of the way in which the healthy functioning of the human body may be affected by the abuse of solvents, tobacco and other drugs

> **aged 14-16** to have opportunities to consider the effects of solvents, alcohol, tobacco and other drugs on the way the human body functions.

Although the National Curriculum does not specify how many hours should be spent on drug education or how it should be delivered, standards have been monitored by HMI (Her Majesty's Inspectorate), who conducted a small number of inspections of health education which included elements of drug education. In future, standards of delivery of education will be monitored by a new Inspectorate system and HMI will operate as part of the Office for Standards in Education (Ofsted) in England and the Office of Her Majesty's Chief Inspector of Schools (OHMCI) in Wales. **It is important that the standards of delivery of health education including drug education are included within the new system.**

5.2.2 Although health education is not in itself a statutory component of the National Curriculum, the National Curriculum Council (NCC) has identified it as a major cross-curricular theme contributing to pupils' personal and social development. The NCC's document "Curriculum Guidance 5: Health Education" was issued to all primary and secondary schools in September 1990 [18] (see Appendix D). It advised that substance misuse was a key area which pupils should study at all stages of their school careers. It also contained guidance on the issues to be covered at each stage and how these might be integrated into the wider curriculum.

5.2.3 The policy of the Education Departments is to stimulate, encourage and support work within schools and the youth service, with a view to ensuring that young people are made aware of the dangers of drug misuse and are equipped with the attitudes and skills they need to resist pressure to misuse them. In line with the advice given in the ACMD's 1984 Prevention Report, DFE (Department for Education) and the Welsh Office have encouraged schools to adopt an approach which sets education on drugs in the broader context of an overall programme of preventive health which emphasises the benefits of a healthy lifestyle and enables young people to make informed and responsible choices. The adoption by schools of a broad, positive approach to health issues is endorsed by professional opinion and practical experience alike as being relevant to the needs of the majority of pupils.

5.2.4 The DFE and the Welsh Office support the development of teaching materials, and provide basic information, where necessary, to all Local Education Authorities (LEAs), schools, teachers and youth workers in England and Wales on the problems of drug abuse and the need to tackle those problems in the context of health education. They also provide financial support to key voluntary organisations for specific activities relating to education about drugs within schools and the youth service.

5.3 The National Level: Northern Ireland

5.3.1 In Northern Ireland the school curriculum for pupils aged 4-16 years includes the cross-curricular theme of health education which aims, among other things, to develop in children a critical awareness of the use, misuse, risks and effects of drugs and other potentially harmful substances; their catastrophic effects on health; and their personal, social and economic implications.

5.3.2 As a cross-curricular theme, health education will not be taught as a distinct subject but rather through the statutory programmes of study for individual subjects in the curriculum. From September 1992, schools were required to include the attainment of the objectives of this theme in the curriculum for all pupils. Although this cross-curricular theme of health education did not become mandatory by law until September 1992, it has been already incorporated into the compulsory programmes of study for individual subjects introduced to date, notably science, and it reinforces existing personal and social education programmes already in existence in schools.

5.3.3 In particular the science programme of study introduces pupils at:

key stage 1 (age 4-8) to ideas about how to keep healthy and about the safe use of medicines

key stage 2 (age 8-11) to the fact that, while all medicines are drugs, not all drugs are medicines; and they should begin to be aware at this stage of the catastrophic effects on health arising from an abuse of drugs

key stage 3 (11-14) pupils study ways in which the healthy functioning of the body may be promoted or disrupted by lifestyle issues and the use and abuse of drugs together with the importance of responsible interpersonal relationships

key stage 4 (14-16) pupils consider the effects of solvents, alcohol, tobacco and other drugs on the way the human body functions and are encouraged to seek out, select and use reference materials from a range of sources and perspectives.

5.3.4 From September 1992, schools were required to make and keep up to date a written statement of curriculum policy including Health Education and to take account of any representations made about that policy.

5.3.5 In addition, the Department of Education for Northern Ireland (DENI) issues circulars of advice and guidance on matters such as drug abuse to Education and Library boards, schools and youth bodies.

5.4 The National Level: Scotland

5.4.1 In Scotland the Scottish Office Education Department (SOED) has the responsibility of coordinating guidance on drug education in schools. Although there is no compulsory national curriculum in Scotland, Scottish Office policy is to encourage schools to tackle drug issues within the context of a comprehensive programme of health and social education. All education authorities in Scotland have programmes of drug education and in all schools there is a designated teacher with responsibility for health education. Within primary schools, health education, including drug misuse, is recognised as a constituent element of environmental studies.

5.4.2 SOED has funded the production and distribution of the drug education package "Drugwise Too". This pack, developed by Strathclyde Regional Council, updates and replaces the successful and widely used "Drugwise 10-14". The new material is aimed at a younger and wider age group (10-14) and has been made available to education authorities and independent schools for distribution to all primary, secondary and special schools. It includes a revised version of the videotape as well as updated materials. To complement the pack SOED, in conjunction with the Health Education Board for Scotland (HEBS) and DFE, has produced and distributed "Drugwise 14-18" to education authorities.

5.4.3 The Scottish Consultative Council on the Curriculum (SCCC) and HEBS have also produced a report "Promoting Good Health" which gives detailed guidance on planning a structure and comprehensive programme of health education for the 10-14 age group, with an accompanying booklet for parents explaining what schools are trying to do and how parents can help. Both have been made available to all primary and secondary schools in Scotland.

5.5 The Regional/District Level

5.5.1 In England and Wales most LEAs from 1986 used education support grants (ESG) from the then Department of Education and Science (DES, now the Department for Education: DFE) and Welsh Office to fund the employment of Drug Education Coordinators (DECs) whose role was to stimulate and support the development of drug education by LEA institutions, schools, colleges and the youth service. From 1990-91 (1989-90 in Wales) the education support grant system was changed to cover wider aspects of preventive health education including alcohol, tobacco and HIV/AIDS as well as drugs, and the LEAs replaced the DECs with Health Education Coordinators (HECs). This new grant, the Grant for Education, Support and Training (GEST) for preventive health education was introduced as a pump-priming exercise for a three year period from April 1990 to March 1993. (In Wales, the programme is continuing, albeit in a slightly different form. Grant is available in 1993/94 under the GEST system for activities to develop Personal and Social Education (PSE) in schools, including health education.) The majority of LEAs now have HECs and many of them play a part in informing and advising schools on the material available, although ultimately the school is responsible for the implementation of courses and materials used. The HECs' role is also to establish networks and to act as focal points for the dissemination of useful information and good practice.

5.5.2 *The GEST funding for preventive health* was examined in a survey by Her Majesty's Inspectorate (HMI) in England in late 1991 [19] whose purpose was to assess the impact of the English GEST programme on the provision for health education in schools, colleges of further education and the youth service. The report concluded that there had been a smooth transition from the ESG funding programme to the GEST funding programme with many of the former DECs appointed to new posts as HECs. This enabled authorities to build on the knowledge and experience acquired by the DECs. The new HECs had shown themselves able to accommodate the wider health education brief and to balance their priorities between drugs, other substances and HIV/AIDS. HECs constituted a major and sometimes the major source of advice and guidance on the policy and practice of health education in LEAs. A strong feature of the work of the HECs was the level of cooperation established with other community agencies who share a common interest in promoting a healthy life-style among young people. Those agencies expressed strongly their appreciation of the contribution made by HECs to the process. The report concluded that the GEST funding had played a valuable role in raising levels of health awareness, equipping staff with the knowledge and skills to develop and implement programmes of education on health matters. A 1989 HEA/MORI survey of health education in England [20] also noted the key role played by HECs. Further information on the work of HECs is contained in appendix E.

5.5.3 *Local authority guidelines on health education:* The above-mentioned HMI report found that specific policies or guidelines on health education existed in a little under half of the authorities in the sample whilst around a quarter of the others either had draft policies or had included a significant health education component in the guidelines issued on personal and social education. The HECs had been a major factor in steering LEAs towards formulating statements on health education or ensuring its place in broader curricular guidelines. HECs were also playing a key role in assisting LEAs and schools in adapting to take account of the inclusion of the health aspects of the National Curriculum.

5.5.4 *Local authority guidelines on the management of drug related incidents:* An HMI inspection of a sample of LEAs in 1988, quoted in the HMI report [19], found that less than half had produced guidelines on the management of drug related incidents in education establishments, but by the time of the HMI report the figure had increased to about 60% of LEAs surveyed. An increase in the reported number of drug related incidents in several of the authorities had encouraged them to formulate such guide-lines or codes of practice. However the quality of the guidelines and nature of the referral procedures advocated differed markedly between LEAs. The more successful guidelines were generally found to be those which had been drafted by HECs in consultation with heads, the police and local drug advisory teams. The consultation process helped to reveal, and often to resolve, some of the problems which might arise.

5.5.5   As it is ultimately the individual school which will have to implement such a policy and every school is different, it is important that policies formulated at local education authority level are done so in close cooperation with schools and community agencies in the area: the policy may need to be flexible enough to let different schools in the area set their own more specific policies according to their pupils' circumstances and needs. In many areas there will be benefit from LEAs and schools co-operating and exchanging ideas at an informal level. (We return to this issue in the next chapter.)

5.5.6 The HMI report [19] mentions that several authorities had noted an increase in drug-related incidents. No mention, however, is made of any attempts to formally monitor such incidents. Despite the difficulty of per-suading schools to participate in such a monitoring scheme, it is clear that unless a problem is monitored or measured, it is difficult to make effective plans for overcoming it. Careful consideration should therefore be given to how this issue could be addressed. Authorities would need to be able to convince schools that maximum confidentiality would be maintained and persuade them of the value of such monitoring. Even in those authorities whose schools claim to have no drug misuse problems, there would be value in authorities having a picture of drug misuse problems outside the school in the community as a whole.

The future of health education coordination
5.5.7 The scheduled end of the GEST programme on preventive health education in March 1993 in England was found by the HMI report [19] to have generated a sense of insecurity which affected long term planning strategies for further development of health education in many authorities. The report recommended that authorities should be looking

more rigorously at ways in which the existing provision for health education could be maintained and enhanced in the post-GEST period. **We believe that good coordination at local authority level is essential to ensure full and effective implementation of a good nationwide system of drug and health education, including (in England and Wales) the National Curriculum drug education element and the guidance contained in the NCC guidance note on health education. This is particularly important at a time when many schools have only begun to implement these new measures. (We return to this point in the next chapter.)**

5.5.8 The transition to grant maintained ("opted-out") schools will not eliminate the need for coordination and exchange of experience between schools themselves and between schools, the local authorities and other agencies such as health education/promotion authorities, charities, the police, youth agencies and so on. And those schools still run by local authorities will continue as before to need a focal point for coordination with the local authority.

5.5.9 To be effective, planning and coordination of services such as the provision of health education must take a long term view. In 1988 a resolution of the European Council and Ministers of Education meeting within the Council on health education in schools [21] called on Member States to "ensure that current plans take into account and in the long-term strengthen health education measures.." and recommended that all schools should implement health education programmes. One of the reasons stated in the document for the issue of this resolution was concern in the EC at "the increase of drug abuse including tobacco and alcohol". Such rising trends in drug misuse can only be effectively com-batted by well co-ordinated, long-term planning and provision of services, of which preventive education is a key element.

5.5.10 We are concerned that the ending of GEST funding for preventive health education will mean that many local authorities will not be able to fund their health education initiatives and HEC posts. Those in the more deprived areas where drugs might be more prevalent may be least able to provide financial resources to continue this work. Although it will be open to Local Authorities to use funds provided for the National

Curriculum as a whole (of which drug education is an element) we fear that drug and health education are in danger of being marginalised by the pressure to concentrate on mainstream subjects. This in turn will mean that schools do not get the expert help, advice and resources they need to implement health and drug education programmes or to develop them effectively. **We feel that more ways must be found to 'earmark' funding for health and drug education if an effective, long-term strategy to improve the health of a growing generation is to be implemented and maintained.**

5.5.11 Furthermore, there is a need to monitor the way in which National Curriculum money is distributed amongst the topics it covers to ensure that funding for the drug education element of the curriculum is not squeezed out. Authorities might benefit from guidelines which include arrangements for monitoring the implementation of drug education programmes in schools. Drug education should be included in the subjects inspected under the new schools inspectorate system.

5.6 The local level - the school itself

5.6.1 The new developments in the education system will mean that schools will gradually acquire greater autonomy and will therefore carry much of the responsibility for planning and implementation of health education programmes along with other subjects in the National Curriculum. Grant maintained schools ("opted-out" schools) will be more like independent schools in that they will not be directly controlled by the local authority. Unlike independent schools (see chapter 6.20) they will still be state-funded and obliged to cover the National Curriculum. Schools will still benefit from co-ordination with local agencies including the local authorities and from informal exchanges with other schools as we emphasised in the preceding section. However, much of the detailed work will be done by the school itself and its managers.

5.6.2 Responsibility for the implementation of health and drugs education rests with the head teacher in consultation with school governors or school board and parents, and, as appropriate, in liaison with the local education authorities. Different communities and schools have different needs. A detailed programme for drug education needs to be adopted at local level by the local education authorities and by the individual schools. This should be preceded by an assessment by the school authorities of the needs of the school community and should involve representatives from all areas of the local community including parents. Schools would benefit from having a designated member of the teaching staff with suitable training to act as health education coordinator within the school and to liaise with the education authorities. In England and Wales currently around 90% of secondary schools and a smaller percentage of primary schools have an identified coordinator responsible for health education in the school. Around 95% of secondary schools now have a specific social and health programme. However in 1989 the HEA/MORI survey of health education in England [20] noted that implementation of health education tended to be an internal school affair with little involvement of governors, parents or LEA advisors, particularly in the case of primary schools.

5.6.3 It is generally found that the 10-14 years period is the crucial age at which experimentation commonly begins although in the case of volatile substances there have been fatalities as young as nine years old. Education needs to start two to three years before the likely age of experimentation. (This is reflected in the requirements of National Curriculum Science for England and Wales and the School Curriculum in Northern Ireland.) There is a case for increasing the coverage of health education in primary schools and for more primary schools to have health education coordinators and specific programmes of health and for personal and social skills training including drug education. Drug education in school should continue up to the end of the school career, and should be delivered regularly and at appropriate stages. We examine the school programme in more detail in the next chapter.

6. FRONT LINE ACTION: THE SCHOOL ITSELF

6.1 The school drug education programme needs to be developed consistently across the school career within the overall context of health education and substance misuse, taking account of age, sex, cultural background and the school environment. It can be addressed in a number of subjects such as science, history and geography, physical education, religious education, drama and even included in first-aid training but it is important that the diversity of subjects under which drugs can be studied does not lead to an inconsistent message to pupils: hence the need for coordinated, planned programmes delivering consistent advice. An example of the substance abuse programme adopted by one school is contained in appendix F.

6.2 The effectiveness of a health education programme can be reinforced by the attitude to health in the school as a whole and among the school staff. Consideration should be given as to whether the school should allow smoking by adults on the school premises or whether alcohol should be served at occasions attended by both staff and pupils. The Scottish policy document, 'Scotland's Health' [4] recognises the influence the school's image can have and includes an undertaking "to discuss with education authorities how they might further encourage schools to exemplify a healthy lifestyle".

6.3 The 1989 HEA/MORI survey of health education in schools in England [20] found that 70% of the secondary schools surveyed had a written health education or PSE policy and most of the remainder had plans to formulate such a policy. Primary schools were found to be much less likely to have a policy in place, with only a third of those surveyed having done so but it was expected that this would rise to cover two thirds as policies were developed. However, primary school policies tended to concentrate on exercise and nutrition, with drugs only being covered in secondary school policies. Many policies were found to be little more than curriculum outlines, but the majority who had policies claimed to monitor their policies in some way, most commonly by feedback from staff but rarely by feedback from pupils. (See section 6.10 on reviewing the programme.) Most schools were aware of the existence of an LEA health education policy but it appeared that LEA policies had only a minor influence on the development of schools' own policies. Although all schools surveyed appeared to have restrictions on smoking, very few had a written policy and only a minority operated an outright ban. Independent schools appeared to have stricter policies on smoking than state schools. (We return to the question of school policies in sections covering welfare and management of drug-related incidents.)

6.4 *Methods and delivery*

Peer groups and television are strong influences on children. They are quick to criticise many forms of education as boring. School drug education needs to take account of this by promoting supervised group discussion and considering peer-led education programmes, by addressing the media and TV representation of drug misuse and by the imaginative use of videos, computer-based learning programmes and other teaching aids. The programme should aim not only to deliver the level of information that the target group of pupils need, but also to involve the pupils themselves in the business of making informed choices. There can be value in involving the older pupils themselves in aspects of the planning and implementation of a drug education programme. This can help them to see the relevance of the programme to them and their everyday life.

6.5 Pupils need to learn the personal skills necessary to make informed choices about their life styles, including communication, assertiveness, handling emotions, interpersonal skills, ways of resisting pressure, team work, role playing and so on. The programme needs to be adapted to the needs of its audience: for a child from a chaotic home environment, health education may seem irrelevant. The programme needs to encompass the needs of such children, helping them to cope with the stresses of their home and daily life and to understand the relevance of the health education lessons.

6.6 We found that programmes which combined a strong pupil participation with careful planning and supervision by qualified teaching staff were better received and appeared to have the best impact. Well-defined peer-led learning schemes incorporated into such programmes stimulated pupils' interest and involvement and may play a valuable role in getting messages across, particularly to older pupils, in a non-didactic (and therefore to them more acceptable) way. Some schemes, set up with broader aims, such as crime prevention panels or student support schemes, provided a valuable framework in which drug misuse could be addressed as part of a school's overall health or personal and social education programmes.

6.7 *Content*

The drug education programme should cover all aspects of substance misuse including alcohol and tobacco and present a consistent approach. Naturally the depth of coverage of the subject needs to be graded in accordance with the age group addressed. Furthermore the emphasis given to different substances needs to reflect the local situation. It is likely to be important to give early emphasis to the dangers of volatile substance abuse, which can kill first-time experimenters, involves a generally younger age group than other drugs and accounts for a higher number of fatalities from abuse than any other misused drug. The education programme needs to address issues such as the role of prescribed medicine in society and the problems that can arise from over-use of prescribed medicine, the medical and social harm arising from drug misuse and the legal framework of drug misuse. Schools need to address the issue of "legalisation" and deliver a consistent message that stresses the harm of drug misuse in any form, regardless of the legal context.

6.8 *Resources - human and materials*

In planning a programme of drug education, schools need to have information on the teaching resources available so that they can select the most appropriate materials for their own needs. They also need a contact point from which they will be able to get that information. They need to consider the resources available to or used by any outside agencies that they may involve in the programme, such as police, the youth service and local drugs agencies, to ensure that materials used in the programme are consistent and coordinated. The Scottish Office policy document "Scotland's Health" [4] identifies this need and has called on the Scottish Consultative Council on the Curriculum and the Health Education Board for Scotland "to work together to establish a national resource centre for health education, upon which teacher training establishments, education authorities, schools and teachers themselves can draw."

6.9   In selecting materials, care needs to be taken to ensure that the materials are practical and easy to use in the school situation and provide adequate guidance to the teacher in the use of the resource material. Teachers may need guidance and training in the use of some materials. (We return to the issue of training in chapter 9).

6.10 *The programme - audit and review*

Schools need to carry out a regular audit of the way in which the school's need for drug education is being met and the delivery of the programme in the context of more general programmes of health, personal and social education.   This should take account of relevant national and local education authority guidelines, such as the curriculum guidance booklet on health education [18] but concentrate on the implementation of the drug education programme in the school itself.   Although, as we discussed in chapter 3, a scientific evaluation of the effect of the drug education programme would be very difficult for a school to carry out, nevertheless there would be merit in including a general review and assessment of the content of the programme, its mode of delivery and its perceived impact on pupils and parents in parallel with the audit.   This review might seek the views of pupils, consider the involvement and role of parents, the provision of staff training, links with the community and so on.   The school might also use the occasion of the audit and review to evaluate its policy on management of drug-related incidents (see later sections).

6.11 *Welfare*

It is important for schools to aim to identify those school pupils who are misusing illegal drugs and volatile substances at the earliest possible stage by encouraging pupils who have problems to come forward for help. The general ethos of the school and the quality of pastoral care will be important factors in a school's ability to persuade pupils with problems to come forward and to assist such pupils. The increasing influence of market forces on the way in which schools are run can result in an "ostrich-like" approach to drug problems by schools - if you can't see it, it isn't there.   This unfortunately can lead to problems being discovered only when they are too bad to ignore and the resultant media interest damaging the image of the school. A carefully planned and presented school policy which stresses the school's pastoral role and its proactive approach to drug and health education can by contrast be a positive marketing tool.

6.12 Such a policy needs to be prepared to deliver help to a pupil who has a substance misuse problem. In such cases schools need to work closely with parents and to encourage them to involve the pupils' GPs. Schools need to be aware of specialist services and youth services and agencies in the area that can offer help and to develop contacts with them, if necessary, to assess whether they would be able to offer appropriate help.

6.13 *Management of drug-related problems*
Schools need a clear and well publicised policy on handling the problem of pupils found possessing, selling or using drugs (including volatile substances, tobacco and alcohol) on school property. The policy needs to be consistently maintained. Schools need to balance the interests of the reputation of the school, the need to protect other pupils and the need to help those who do misuse drugs. Having a clear and consistent policy that has been discussed by all those involved in the school including parents can help to address these problems. If such policies were to become established practice in schools and LEAs, this would also help to remove the stigma associated with addressing the issue of drug misuse. Such a policy clearly needs to include disciplinary measures to be taken, especially with regard to pupils found dealing with illegal drugs, but as the overlap between pupils selling or sharing their drugs among their peers ie "dealers" and "pupils with drug misuse problems" may be indistinct, the need to help pupils with a drug misuse problem should not be overlooked in such cases. Permanent exclusion or expulsion should be seen as a last resort as it only transfers the problem.

[Note: In Scotland, the term 'exclusion' is used for temporary banning of a pupil from school and 'expulsion' for permanent exclusion. In England the term expulsion is not used and instead authorities use the terms 'temporary' 'intermediate' or 'permanent' exclusion.]

6.14 The need for a clear policy on dealing with drug misuse was highlighted, for example, by a recent Department of Education for Northern Ireland (DENI) circular issued to schools, colleges and youth groups on drug education which stated:

"It is essential that there should exist clear guidelines and procedures for staff who may have to deal with cases of possible misuse of illegal drugs".

The circular went on to recommend that school and college governing bodies should draw up policies regarding drug misuse outlining procedures to be followed when drug-related incidents occur and guidance for dealing with parents, outside agencies, the police and, where relevant, the press. It also recommended that schools and colleges should have a designated member of staff to take responsibility for co-ordination of arrangements and likewise that education boards should have an officer for co-ordinating action on drug misuse in all educational establishments. [DENI circular no. 1992/2 of 3 January 1992.]

6.15 If the education authority has already formulated a policy on the management of drug related incidents, schools need to coordinate with them to ensure that the policy is appropriate for the individual school. If there is no education authority policy, individual schools might consider encouraging the authority to consult schools in the area and formulate an agreed policy. The HMI report on GEST funding in England [19] found that many schools were not aware of their LEA guidelines or found them unhelpful or unworkable, which led to an inconsistent or erratic response on the part of schools in the management of drug-related incidents. Pupils were immediately excluded in one school for being associated with drug misuse but allowed to remain in attendance and given support and counselling in another. The report concluded that:

"Discussions between LEAs and their schools, colleges and youth service and within the schools themselves would help to achieve a more considered and informed response on the few but growing number of occasions that drug misuse has to be faced."

6.16 The referral of children under 16 years to drug agencies who may not be equipped to handle younger clients is a problem that has been highlighted by HECs. Any referral to an agency needs to take careful account of the age of the child and whether that agency can offer appropriate assistance.

6.17 The school policy would need to address the issue of whether to contact the police. Teachers are not under a legal obligation to report **all** incidents relating to illegal drugs to the police. However, under section 8 of the Misuse of Drugs Act 1971, it is an offence for someone "concerned in the management of any premises" to **knowingly** permit the production or supply of any controlled drug on the premises or the preparation or smoking of opium or cannabis on the premises. Furthermore a teacher's employer might object if a teacher does not disclose information about a drug related incident. If a teacher confiscates drugs from a pupil, or finds drugs, s/he should immediately hand the drugs to someone in authority, for example a police officer, or else destroy the drug, for example, by flushing it down a lavatory, preferably in the presence of an authoritative witness. In any case of doubt, a teacher might consider consulting the school police liaison officer by presenting the problem as a hypothetical case: ie "What would you advise if....". Before taking action, it is important that a teacher establishes what the evidence is and does not react simply to accusations. If drugs are found not physically on a person but somewhere else such as in a locker, someone else might have put them there. The school's policy should give teachers clear guidance on contacting the police. It is helpful for schools to develop close relationships with their police liaison officers and seek their advice when formulating a school policy on the management of drug-related incidents. (We return to the role of police in schools in a later section.)

6.18 Closely linked with the issues raised by contact with the police is the difficult question of confidentiality. A clear policy will help to resolve these difficulties by setting out how teachers should balance the need to help a pupil with the issue of confidentiality. Before embarking on a discussion, a teacher could explain to the pupil in question what the ground rules are.

6.19 *Procedures adopted* for the management of drug-related problems therefore need to address the following points:

- informing parents

- the nature of measures which schools might implement for first and later offences, taking into account the type of drug involved and the distinction between 'legal' substances (eg alcohol, tobacco, volatile substances) and illegal drugs, the seriousness of the problem, where it took place, the role of the pupil(s) involved, their home backgrounds and the cultural/community environment

- the circumstances under which exclusion/expulsion would apply and what other measures would be taken along with it

- the procedure in the case of pupils found taking drugs or intoxi-cated with drugs on school premises: the school needs to ensure that the pupil is given adequate care and is taken home safely and the school and other pupils need to be protected

- the situation with regard to the law; liaison with the police

- access to specialist advice for pupils with drug problems and referral where appropriate to other agencies, including local drug agencies, social services, and consultation between agencies to reach agreement on procedures to be adopted

- confidentiality.

LEA statements on the management of drug related incidents could usefully be framed in terms of the type of questions schools should ask themselves in determining the appropriate action to take.

6.20 *The position of independent schools*
In England and Wales, private or independent schools which do not receive funding from the State do not have to comply with the National Curriculum, but they receive information and guidance about it from the Department for Education and the Welsh Office and most of them choose to follow the National Curriculum fairly closely. In Scotland where there is no National Curriculum, the Scottish Office gives identical advice to

both private and state-supported schools and (as in England and Wales) all are currently inspected by HMI. The principles of drug education apply as much to independent schools as to any other school but they face some particular problems:

- They rely on market forces for their intake and are therefore particularly sensitive to publicity about drugs problems. In some cases this can lead to a problem not being tackled until it has become a major (and very public) upheaval.

- Pupils may be from wealthy backgrounds and have the money to buy drugs.

- Many such schools are boarding schools and therefore pupils are away from parental influence: peer pressure may have a greater effect.

6.21 It follows from this that there is an even more pressing need for such schools to have a clear policy on drugs, together with a programme of drugs education, and to seek to identify and tackle problems as early as possible. The 1989 HEA/MORI survey of health education in England (20), whilst noting that provision of designated health coordinators in schools was generally on the increase, also commented that independent schools were "noticeably less likely to have a health coordinator, just as they were less likely to have a health education policy". It was also found that staff at independent schools were less likely to have attended health education courses.

6.22 On the other hand, an independent school which can advertise the quality of the pastoral care it provides, the school ethos and its positive approach to personal, social and health education should put itself in a strong position in the market place (see section 6.11).

7. LIAISON WITH THE COMMUNITY

7.1 *Parents*

The involvement and support of parents is an important factor in ensuring the effectiveness of any messages about drug education: if school and parents convey radically different messages to children, they are likely to reject one or other or both sets of messages. The role of parent governors (or in Scotland parent members of school boards) is particularly important in the formulations of a school's strategy on drug education. Parents need to be informed and involved at every stage of the implementation, development and evaluation of a drug education programme. The Parent Teacher Association (PTA) can be a useful forum for exchanging views. Health education coordinators (HECs) can also play an important role in involving parents. The HMI report [17] found that in one LEA a series of 24 parents' meetings arranged by the HEC on the theme of young people and drug misuse reached a total of 1,600 parents. The report concluded that:

"Both governors and parents had generally valued those occasions, not least because of the informal style of group work adopted by HECs and the serious attempts made to relate the topic to the needs and local circumstances of the audiences. The meetings had allowed adults to explore some entrenched attitudes and beliefs on health matters and to become better acquainted with the work children undertake in their schools' health education programmes."

7.2 Parents should be encouraged to take an active and involved role in the school's health education programme. Where appropriate they could be invited to attend and/or participate in a health education session with pupils.

7.3 Schools whose premises are also used for adult education courses can use the opportunity to offer adults whose children attend the school information about the school's health education and drug education programme. The wider role played by the school as a centre for activity in the community was recognised, for example, in the policy document "Scotland's Health" [4] which noted that: "The policies followed in schools in relation to health education can therefore be a useful source of information for the wider community and have a positive influence on general attitudes to health".

7.4 Drug education needs to be explained to parents with care. Parents may be afraid that their child might be harmed by knowledge about drugs. They need to be reassured that the drug education programme is delivered in a controlled and supervised environment and in stages appropriate to the age and experience of the child. They need to understand the aims and objectives of the programme: firstly to prevent drug misuse and secondly to identify and protect from further harm those who have already experimented with drugs. Parents may be unaware of the possibility that their child might be exposed to drugs in their area and therefore of the importance of a good school-based prevention programme. Parents who tragically lose a child for example as a result of volatile substance abuse often say that it never occurred to them that their child might do such a thing. These dangers need to be made clear to parents as well as children. Parents need guidance in how to recognise signs that their child might be misusing substances and how to seek help. Schools can play a role in assisting parents. Parents may be reluctant to get involved in drug education out of embarrassment or fear that people might think they have a "problem child" or the school has a "drug problem". Approaching the subject in the context of a health education programme and providing clear information explaining the aims of the programme can help to overcome such embarrassment: a tactful approach can help remove the stigma from drug education.

7.5 *Community involvement in schools* should be fostered to promote a consistent message inside and outside school and to give support to teachers in providing information and expertise. Voluntary organisations undertaking specific projects relating to drug education in schools need to work closely with and under the guidance of the school teaching staff and in the context of the school's overall programme of drug education. Opportunities in the community for sport, recreation, leisure and employment need to be tied in with the teaching of decision-making skills in the classroom about finding alternatives to drug misuse. Schools need to be aware of the range of agencies and services available in their area, including primary healthcare services, which can help in developing the school drug education programme. The LEA Health Education Coordinator (HEC) and designated staff in the school can play a key role in ensuring good liaison between the school and other agencies in the community. The HMI report [19] noted that most authorities surveyed had established good co-operation between the health promotion officers of the District Health Authority and the HECs and also that Home Office Drug Prevention Teams established in various parts of the country with the aim of encouraging the local community to generate their own ideas to combat drug misuse had provided support for school-based drug education.

7.6 *The role of the police in liaising with schools*

Many schools have found it helpful to draw upon the expertise of the police in both the development and delivery of drugs and wider health programmes. In most authorities, local constabularies have a schools involvement programme and many have written manuals on various topics. The programme has three main aspects: health education, the role of the police and citizenship. Police liaison officers visit schools and work closely with local health education coordinators, teachers and pupils on a range of safety and crime prevention initiatives including drug education. This practice is set out in a published HMI Survey "Our Policeman: Good Practice in Police/School Liaison" [22].

7.7 Notwithstanding the potential conflict between, on the one hand, the contribution police officers can make towards educating pupils in relation to drugs and, on the other, their responsibility to uphold the law in relation to the use or possession of controlled drugs, it is clear that particularly effective links have developed in many areas. Provided the police work in co-operation with schools and HECs as part of a planned programme of work, they can make a valuable contribution towards the development and delivery of local drugs education. They are also particularly well-placed to advise teachers and parents and to contribute to drug-related in-service training courses, by providing specialist knowledge on the local drugs situation, clarifying legal issues and explaining police practice and referral procedures.

7.8 Secondary school police liaison officers are often drawn from police, youth and community units who have volunteered for and are specially trained for the work. In London, for example, some of this training takes place at teacher training college, involving a 5 day course. There is a move to use specially trained officers at primary school level. Some HECs and Health promotion officers also offer training days for such officers on specific health issues.

7.9 It has been found that the police presentation was more effective when delivered to small informal groups and as part of the overall programme. Guidelines to police liaison officers generally aim to keep them up to date with substance misuse trends, the National Curriculum and the need to liaise with health/personal and social education coordinators in the school and to ensure that their presentation fits in with the relevant project or curriculum work.

(We return to the subject of training in Chapter 9.)

8. DRUG EDUCATION FOR CHILDREN IN CARE

8.1 It has to be recognised that children being looked after in public care are vulnerable to a range of detrimental influences as they get older, of which drug misuse is only one. These children need proactive training on how to combat these hazards. For this reason the 1989 Children Act guidance on the regulations relating to the residential care of children makes clear that programmes of health education and health care should be part of the package offered to such children. However, because of concerns about the quality of management and practice in children's homes, as described in the Utting Report "Children in the Public Care, HMSO 1991", and in the Welsh Office report "Accommodating Children" published in the following year, the implementation of effective health education programmes in this setting still requires much developmental work.

8.2 Relevant recommendations in the Utting Report relating to drug education are:

- Individual homes to include programmes of health education and health care in their statements of objectives (Paragraph 3.24);

- Care authorities to secure with health authorities local agree-ments for providing psychological and psychiatric support for children in care (Paragraph 3.25);

- The Department of Health to discuss with the Department of Education and Science (now the Department for Education) the feasibility of guidance to education authorities about the educational needs of children in care (Paragraph 3.27);

- Care authorities to make full use of youth and educational services in devising constructive programmes of leisure activities, and participate in programmes of crime prevention (Paragraphs 3.28 and 3.44);

- Department of Health to give priority to residential care in the first review of the adequacy of child care training under section 83 of the Act (Paragraph 5.18);

-   Department of Health to re-emphasise the priority for residential child care staff under the 1992-93 Training Support Programme (Paragraph 5.18).

8.3 Children in public care are not as easily accessible as children living with their families and in regular school attendance. Moving into accommodation provided by a local authority, even when undertaken with good planning, will always cause some dislocation to supportive services. It is a regulatory requirement that children being placed in children's homes or foster homes under the Children Act are medically examined, although a child over the age of 16 has the right to refuse. This requirement would be in line with the terms of the new GP contract in which the child would be invited to attend a registration health check. Part of this check involves questioning about present and/or past use of alcohol, volatile substances and drugs (both prescribed and illicit). This opportunity could then be used to identify any problems and a plan drawn up to assist the child. Interventions would mainly be from a harm minimisation standpoint, if ongoing substance misuse or previous substance misuse is identified, but would also include prevention strategies to provide information on the dangers of substance misuse and the skills needed to resist pressure to experiment. Unfortunately placements often change in an unplanned way and further dislocation may occur, with educational and health care continuity becoming problematic. For these reasons the logistics of effective health education programmes for children in care are not straightforward.

8.4 The Education Reform Act 1988 which requires children of statutory school age in England and Wales to follow the National Curriculum does not apply to children in care, other than to those who attend mainstream schools for their education. There is consequently no assurance that the component of health and drugs education which is covered in the National Curriculum subjects will be provided for these children. The planned and unplanned changes which occur in children's circumstances while placed in care and the widely differing range of provision in care establishments would make longitudinal planning of a standardised health education programme difficult to implement. It may be that the only way to ensure that children with the most disrupted childhoods receive the necessary input is to devise education programmes in children's homes which include an irreducible element of health and drugs education. The organisation and delivery of the programme would need to take account of individual children's knowledge, understanding and experience. Such a curriculum requirement would have implications for the health and drugs related in-service training of teachers and residential social workers in children's homes, and may need a support input from health personnel.

9. TRAINING

9.1 If drug education is to be effective, it follows that staff delivering education must receive adequate training. This is vital not only to ensure the quality of provision of drug education but also to give the providers - the staff - the back-up and confidence to ensure that they and what they teach has credibility in the eyes of young people. In keeping with the recommendation of our Training Report [6], we believe that, where possible, such training should be delivered within a wider substance misuse context to cover illegal drugs, volatile substances, alcohol and tobacco. It also needs to address teachers' own attitudes to substance misuse in order to help them feel able to tackle the issue with young people. Such training may be conveniently placed within a health education training course.

9.2 The 1988 EC resolution on health education [21] called on Member States "to develop teacher training for health education both at initial and in-service levels, so that:

-   teachers from all disciplines are sensitized to their potential role as promoters of health education,

-   teachers in particularly relevant disciplines receive adequate specialized training

-   those responsible for the management of schools are made aware of the need to promote health education concepts in practice in schools."

Furthermore the 1990 declaration of the World Ministerial Summit to Reduce Demand for Drugs and to Combat the Cocaine Threat, to which the UK was a signatory, required that teachers in relevant disciplines should receive appropriate specialised training at both initial and in-service levels.

9.3 *Initial Teacher Training*
Most teachers are trained by means of either a four year undergraduate course leading to a Bachelor of Education (BEd) degree or a Bachelor of

Arts (BA)/Bachelor of Science (BSc) degree with Qualified Teacher Status or a one-year postgraduate course leading to a Postgraduate Certificate in Education (PGCE). In addition, in England and Wales the Government has encouraged the development of a variety of new types of initial teacher training (ITT) courses, including the Articled Teacher Scheme (a two-year school-based PGCE), the Licensed Teacher Scheme (involving on-the-job training), two and three year BEds and two year PGCEs. The Council for the Accreditation of Teacher Education advises the Secretary of State for Education on the approval or otherwise of ITT courses. All courses require the approval of the Secretary of State and to gain this approval must meet the course criteria set out in DFE circular 24/89. This circular also draws attention to the above-mentioned EC resolution on health education [21] and requires training institutions to take account of it in drawing up courses for approval. In Scotland teacher training courses are accredited by the General Training Council for Scotland (GTC) with whom all teachers in Scotland must be registered.

9.4 Upon completion of their initial training courses, all teachers will be expected to deliver the requirements of the National Curriculum (except in Scotland where the National Curriculum does not apply). This means that all primary-phase courses and secondary-phase courses for subject specialists must address those aspects of drug and health education now included in the programmes of study for National Curriculum science.

9.5 In addition, the primary course criteria require that students should be aware of health education and incorporate it in their teaching. They should also understand the purpose and practice of pastoral care and counselling and be aware of other agencies such as the health services which have a role to play in preventing the misuse of drugs.

9.6 By September 1994, secondary courses will be required to meet new criteria set out in DFE circular 9/92. These require that students should develop a working knowledge of their pastoral duties and a readiness to promote the moral and spiritual well being of pupils. Secondary ITT students will now spend an increased amount of time in schools, giving them an opportunity to observe any drug education work which is being undertaken in their placement schools.

9.7 In Scotland, health education is a compulsory element of all pre-service teacher training courses. The courses include training related to drug misuse, alcohol and smoking. The position in Northern Ireland is similar.

9.8 We believe it is important that teachers are made aware of the principles and need for drug education early in their course of training as messages learnt in initial training can influence attitudes later in the career. Sufficient emphasis should be laid on drug education in initial training courses to ensure that it is seen as an important element of a child's health education and personal development and not a minority specialist subject. If schools are to play an increasingly important role in providing ITT and on-the-job training, those schools must have a good drug education programme in place so that the trainee teacher is able to learn about drug education.

9.9 We found that many institutions which provide teacher-training offer specific training in health education, although the extent may vary considerably between institutions. Courses generally include something on fitness, sex education and child protection but work specifically on drug education is less common. Few students are trained to recognise the signs of drug misuse amongst their pupils or how to deal with such cases. Students, mainly secondary specialists, can often take an elective course on health education, usually varying in length from 6 to 45 hours, although only a minority of students choose to do so. Primary specialists generally follow a core provision which includes elements of health education.

9.10 *In-service training*
The professional development of teachers does not, of course, end with initial training. Throughout their careers, teachers need opportunities to revise, update and enhance their skills and sometimes to learn new ones. In the light of the major changes arising from the implementation of the National Curriculum, effective in-service training is now more important than ever. Responsibility for INSET (In-Service Training) rests with individual LEAs as the major employers of teachers at present. LEAs are best placed to identify and respond to training needs in the light of local

needs and circumstances. INSET covers a wide range of provision from short school-focused initiatives through to longer courses at teachers' centres and substantial award-bearing long courses provided by Higher Education Institutions.

9.11 In 1987 the then Department of Education and Science (DES) introduced a programme of specific grant support for in-service training (INSET) for education professionals about drug misuse. In Wales a parallel scheme was introduced by the Welsh Office in 1989. Between 1987 and 1990 over 100,000 training course places were provided for teachers, advisers and youth workers. From 1990 the training eligible for grant was extended to cover wider aspects of preventive health education about alcohol, tobacco, HIV and AIDS as well as drug education. In Scotland a national programme of in-service training courses aimed primarily at guidance and senior staff in secondary schools and community education workers was mounted in 1985. A specific grant scheme was established in 1986 to encourage drug-related courses. This has since been extended to cover all aspects of health education. In Northern Ireland the in-service training programmes include Health Education and advisory and support staff are employed to assist schools in this area and to keep them alert to the dangers of drug misuse.

9.12 In England and Wales, from 1990, the grant support for INSET was provided from the GEST funding scheme. The HMI report on the scheme in England [19] concluded that levels of take-up of INSET in health education had been impressive but there were signs that the momentum might not be sustainable. Some LEAs had devolved GEST funding for INSET to schools and many schools found that they had inadequate funding to cover the release of teachers for training on health-related matters. Health Education Co-ordinators (HECs) had played a key role in contributing to LEA programmes of INSET health education courses. The report estimated that about 50% of primary and 80% of secondary schools had been represented at LEA health education training courses. Much of the training was good quality, well-planned to meet individual needs and with a strong element of evaluation written into the programme.

9.13 The report went on to note that, as teachers found it increasingly difficult to be released to attend centrally organised courses, the HECs played an important role in supporting teachers in the classroom and in training courses run within the school. Many HECs produced packs of materials, some of which were later taken up and published by national organisations.

Schools: staff training

9.14 In the emerging new education system, in-service training within schools is likely to play an increasingly important role. In putting together programmes of drug education, schools need to take account of their existing pool of skills and to assess the need for further training. Teachers delivering drug education need to have the confidence to deliver consistent and clear messages about drugs. Their training therefore needs to include all the social, medical and legal issues relating to drug misuse that could arise. They should also be equipped to consider matters of welfare, school policy on discipline, contact with parents and outside agencies, and handling confidentiality. Where a specific training package has been chosen by a school, staff delivering the package need to be trained in its use. Time needs to be set aside for in-service training and provision in the school budget for staff cover for teachers on in-service training.

9.15 An appropriate level of training, information and guidance needs to be provided not only to the teaching staff delivering drug education but also to all other teaching and non-teaching staff involved in the school community, including governors, managers, welfare personnel, catering staff and so on in accordance with their role in the school community. The increasing importance of school governors in managing schools makes their training needs all the more important. This should also include information and guidance to parents and to professionals invited into the school to take part in a drug education programme, such as police liaison officers, to ensure that the messages from them are consistent and coordinated with the school's drug programme. The importance of the position of teachers and other adults involved in the school as role models for the children should be emphasised. If the school has a designated and trained teacher in charge of health and/or personal and social education he or she can play a valuable role in providing information and guidance for other staff.

9.16 *Police training* It may be beneficial for certain in-service training courses on drug education to be open not just to teachers but also to other adults who may be involved in drug education, particularly police for whom it can form part of their community training programme. The use of school INSET days which include the participation of the police is one way to achieve this.

9.17 *Non-statutory organisations* In addition to government agencies there are a number of charitable organisations that can be a useful source of information, guidance and training for school staff. A list of some of these is contained in appendix C.

10. CONCLUSIONS AND RECOMMENDATIONS

10.1 In this final section we wish to emphasise our belief that no amount of abstract recommendations will by itself be of any worth as a basis for making a school-based drug prevention programme actually work and deliver the hoped-for benefits. What is needed to back our recommendations is a commitment to making high quality classroom drug education a tangible reality on a national scale. Only a country-wide effort, adequately resourced, backed by an enhanced system of teacher training, can give any hope of success. In addition, teachers need to be given encouragement and time to engage in this training while the system itself should be monitored and regularly reviewed. Half-hearted efforts can offer no prospect of success and the inevitably poor outcome will reinforce pessimistic expectations. We outline below under headings what we see as constituting the needed strategy to ensure that school-based drug education is indeed being taken seriously, with a commitment to making it work.

A NATIONAL STRATEGY FOR DRUG EDUCATION

10.2 A clearly articulated overall national strategy on school-based drug education building on the National Curriculum and existing provisions must be established as the framework for supporting local action.

10.3 This strategy should integrate activity at the three levels: nationally, locally and at the level of the individual school. The individual school as a community must be the fundamental unit for a national strategy on school-based drug education. The strategy should take as its basis the aim and principles we recommend in chapter 4.

10.4 However the planning and implementation of the necessary educational responses will necessitate partnership between pupils, teachers, parents, governors and the wider community. Support for this partnership must be provided at LEA (or its equivalent) level and at national level. Excellent local practice in one geographical area or in one school will be insufficient unless mechanisms exist to support the replication of good practice nationwide. A national strategy should make good use of the considerable existing skills and experience within the statutory and non-statutory field but should also aim to improve the level of coordination and raise standards throughout the country. Some additional resources will be required but we believe that relatively moderate extra funding carefully deployed will strengthen the total system and secure cost-effective use of existing resources.

ACTION AT NATIONAL LEVEL

MEASURING THE EXTENT OF DRUG MISUSE AMONG SCHOOL-AGE CHILDREN

10.5 Without adequate data on the prevalence and trends in school-age drug misuse, the development of an effective prevention strategy will be fundamentally handicapped. It will be impossible to know whether the situation is improving or deteriorating, either generally or in relation to particular age groups, geographical regions or use of particular drugs, and it will not be possible to set objective targets. **Regular national surveys** should be carried out covering data such as the **age of onset, once-ever** or **regular/frequent drug misuse, attitudes** to and **exposure** to drugs. This would enable national targets to be set just as other targets have been set in the Government White Paper on the Health of the Nation [4]. Samples should be big enough to allow **regional breakdown** and breakdown by **age and sex**. More detailed **local studies** would enhance this picture and inform local planning and provision of services.

EVALUATION OF DRUG EDUCATION

10.6 In parallel with surveys on the extent and nature of drug misuse among school-age children, there is a need for more research into the nature of effective drug education programmes and how they can be evaluated in the context of any overall prevention strategy. Information and experience gained from this research can then by used to plan, inform and review the education programme at all three levels, national, local and school.

GUIDING PRINCIPLES

10.7 The following principles should guide the development of a national strategy on school-based drug education:

NATIONAL STANDARDS AND GUIDELINES need to be established and regularly reviewed as to what constitutes good practice in school-based education. The nature of the drug problem varies over time and geographically. **Guidelines** should be **flexible** enough to allow for local circumstances but **specific targets** should be set which are capable of audit. **National inspections** of schools should include the provision of drug education. The delivery of drug education should also be **monitored** and **audited locally** by local authorities and the schools themselves.

DRUG EDUCATION IN CONTEXT Drug education and education about other forms of substance misuse should be linked with other aspects of health and personal development. Drug misuse sets special problems, but the pupil should integrate consideration of these problems with thinking and learning about wider aspects of respect for his or her health, learning to care about him/herself and acquiring the capacity to make responsible choices.

METHODS

Programmes for drug education should take account of the objectives and principles outlined in chapter **4**, and aim to support the pupil in making healthy choices rather than take a didactic stance. *This recommendation is fundamental to the overall approach to drug education which this working group supports.* Didactic approaches which fail to respect the pupil's own responsibility for developing personal skills will undercut the active involvement which is essential to this type of work.

SETTING TARGETS

10.8 An integrated national strategy must focus on defining and achieving targets in relation to, for example:

- **implementation of school drug education programmes;**

- **teacher training;**

- **school drug policies;**

- **involvement of parents**;

- **the reduction of national prevalence of drug misuse among children of school age.**

Emphasis must be placed on the definition of *specific goals* and *monitoring* of their achievement. Central government should take responsibility for ensuring that a national strategy is *implemented, adequately supported* and *audited*.

ACTION AT LEA OR REGIONAL LEVEL

10.9 **The implementation of the national strategy** should be coordinated at an LEA, local or regional level. Schools will require continued assistance in provision of appropriate teacher training, provision of and advice on teaching materials and advice on formulation and implementation and auditing of school-based drug education policies and programmes. With the cessation of central funding for Health Education Coordinators in England, we recommend that LEAs should determine their strategy and resourcing level to keep the necessary support in place and authorities should report annually to education departments on the provisions made.

10.10 Authorities should work with schools in drawing up *clear and consistent policies on drug education and management of drug related incidents in schools* in their area. Where possible, the nature and frequency of drug-related incidents should be monitored so that appropriate levels of response can be **planned, implemented** and **measured**. In monitoring incidents, care should be taken to ensure confidentiality.

ACTION AT THE SCHOOL LEVEL

10.11 *Every school*, both primary and secondary, should be encouraged to review its response to drug misuse and ensure that a drug education programme is implemented and monitored.

- One or more members of staff should be identified and trained to take lead responsibility for facilitating the planning and implementation of drug education in school.

- The school should ensure that any pupil who encounters problems related to drug misuse has an identified person or person(s) to whom s/he can turn to for confidential advice.

- The school should have an *explicit policy* on the management of drug related incidents. Alternatives to permanent exclusion/expulsion should be preferred where possible.

- The school should consult its parent/teacher association, assist in raising the level of parental awareness of drug misuse, and seek to involve parents in implementing the school drug education programme.

- Every school should instigate a mechanism for auditing the extent and quality of its drug prevention activities on an annual basis and include this audit in a report to the school governors or board.

- The school should aim to support the concept of a healthy and caring environment in all its activities.

THE TRAINING OF TEACHERS IN DRUG EDUCATION

Initial training

10.12 There is a need for recognised courses and consistent national standards of provision of training at initial training level. Minimal training expectations should be defined, mechanisms should be put in place to ensure that such training is made available and the prestige of such work should be enhanced and related to career prospects. Training provision should be reviewed and monitored periodically.

In-service training

10.13 As for initial training, there is a need for a coordinated approach which sets national standards and minimal training expectations and which sets up mechanisms for ensuring that in-service training is provided and monitored. All schools, both primary and secondary, should have a trained coordinator (see earlier) who can take a lead role in delivering drug education to children and in enhancing the skills of other teachers across the school. There is merit in considering opening in-service courses for teachers to others who play a part in the drug education programme such as police officers.

10.14 Information and guidance on drugs and the school's programme and policies should be provided at an appropriate level to all adults involved in the school community.

THE NATIONAL STRATEGY

10.15 *The national strategy on drug education needs to be part of an overall national demand reduction strategy which encourages community action and positive alternatives to drug misuse. The planning and provision of such strategies needs to be based on a long-term view: influencing today's pupils so that, as tomorrow's parents, they will contribute to healthier and more informed attitudes towards their own, their children's and society's use of drugs.*

436pwg.kl9

APPENDIX A

WORKING GROUP ON PREVENTION

Membership since 1991 including co-opted members:

Professor G Edwards (Chairman) - Chairman, National Addiction Centre, Institute of Psychiatry, London

Mrs J Barlow - Projects Manager, Aberlour Childcare Trust, Scotland

Dr W B Clee - General Medical Practitioner, Wales

Mr D S Coleman - former Director of Nursing Services (Psychiatry) now working for the Office of the Health Service Commissioner for England, London

Mrs N Gibbes - Headteacher, Warwick Park Secondary School, London

Professor D G Grahame-Smith - the Chairman of the Advisory Council is an ex-officio member of the Working Group

Mr J L Kay - Managing Director, Healthwise Ltd, Liverpool

Mr A Ramsay - Regional Adviser in Health Education, Strathclyde Regional Council, Scotland

Mr D Turner - Director SCODA (Standing Conference on Drug Abuse), London

Co-opted Members

Mr M Airs - Principal Education Officer (Youth Service), Bedford

Dr N Dorn - ISDD (Institute for the Study of Drug Dependence), London

Ms N Evans - Director, Re-Solv, Staffordshire

Miss M Haydn-Jones - Health Education Advisory Teacher, Wales

Mr J Lee - Chief Executive, TACADE (The Advisory Council on Alcohol and Drug Education), Manchester

Ms A Marshall - Director, ADFAM, London

Mr R Odd - Head of Practice Division, Royal Pharmaceutical Society, London

Dr J Ramsey - Research Fellow, Department of Public Health Services, St. George's Hospital Medical School, London

Chief Supt P Stevens (until October 1992) and **Chief Supt C Benn** (from October 1992) - Community Involvement and Crime Prevention, Metropolitan Police with the assistance of **Inspector Paul Wotton**, Youth Affairs Branch, Metropolitan Police

Mr R Twinn - Director, Group 4 Remand Services Ltd, North Humberside

Mr P Walker - Headteacher, The Abbey School, Kent

Secretary:	Ms K Lidbetter
Assistant Secretary:	Mr P Jones (until December 1991)
	Mr G Lamb (December 1991-June 1992)
	Mr I Cheeseman (from June 1992)
Assisted by:	Miss J K Woodhouse

Officials:

Home Office:

Mr L P Wright (until June 1992)

Mr P R C Storr (from June 1992)

Mr A Norbury

Miss J Mott

Dr M Ramsay

Department of Health:

Ms C Moriarty

Miss M Jackman

Mrs F Wheeler

Scottish Office Home and Health Department

Mrs L Brownlee

Scottish Office Education Department

Mr I Strachan

Department for Education

Mr A B Thompson

Welsh Office

Miss L Rolfe

Northern Ireland DHSS

Mr P M Green (until June 1992)

Mr E B McConkey (from June 1992)

Department of Trade and Industry

Mr J Walker

Department of Employment

Ms A Orr

HM Inspectorate of Schools

Mr D F Lewis, OBE

APPENDIX B

References

1.   Prevention: Report of the Advisory Council on the Misuse of Drugs.
      HMSO Publication, 1984
      ISBN 0 11 340794 7

2. (a) Statistics of Drug Addicts Notified to the Home Office, United
        Kingdom, 1991. Issue 692 published by the Home Office
        ISSN 0143 6384
        19 March 1992

   (b) Statistics of Drug Seizures and Offenders Dealt with, United
        Kingdom, 1991.
        Issue 25/92 ISBN 0143 6384

3.   Choice and Diversity: A New Framework for Schools Produced by
      the Department for Education (DFE) and the Welsh Office, 1992.
      HMSO ISBN 0-10-120212-1

4. (a) The Health of the Nation: A Strategy for Health in England.
        Produced by the Department of Health, 1992.
        HMSO ISBN 0-10-119862-0

   (b) Scotland's Health: A Challenge to Us All. Produced by the Scottish
        Office, 1992.
        HMSO Publication
        ISBN 0 11 4942 18 8

   (c) Plan for action 3: The Agenda for 1992-94. Published by the Health
        Promotion Authority for Wales (June 1992)
        ISBN 1 85687 037 5

5.   Treatment and Rehabilitation: Report of the Advisory Council on
      the Misuse of Drugs
      HMSO Publication, 1982
      ISBN 0 11 320821 9

6. Problem Drug Use: A Review of Training: Report by the Advisory Council on the Misuse of Drugs
HMSO Publication, 1990
ISBN 0 11 340976 1

7. Drinking, Drug Taking and Deviance among Young People: Paper presented to Health in Europe Conference, University of Edinburgh 1992, Newcombe, R, Measham, F and Parker, H.

8. Adolescent Drug Use in Wales
Smith C and Nutbeam D
British Journal of Addiction 1992.
87 pp 227-233

9. Crime, Alcohol, Drugs and Leisure: A Survey of 13,437 young people at school in Mid Glamorgan: produced by the Mid Glamorgan Social Crime Prevention Unit 1991

10. National Evaluation of Drug Education in Scotland Coggans, N, Shewan, D, Henderson, M, Davies, J and O'Hagen, F.
Centre of Occupational and Health Psychology
University of Strathclyde, 1989

11. "Tomorrow's Young Adults: 9-15 Year Olds Look At Alcohol, Drugs, Exercise and Smoking", HEA/MORI 1989

12. Drug Misuse in Britain: National Audit of drug misuse statistics:
ISDD 1991
ISBN 0 94883006 9

13. Contributions of Drug Epidemiology to the Field of Drug Abuse Prevention, Johnston, L D (1991) in C G Leukefeld and W J Bukoski (eds), Drug Abuse Prevention Intervention Research: Methodological Isses. NIDA Research Monograph 107. US Department of Health and Human Services, Rockville, Maryland. pp57-80

14.   Assessing Effectiveness of Drug Abuse Prevention: Implementation Issues Relevant to Long-Term Effects and Replication, Hawkins, J D, Abbott, R, Catalano, R F, and Gillmore M R   (1991) in C G Leukefeld and W J Bukoski (eds.), Drug Abuse Prevention Intervention Research: Methodological Issues. NIDA Research Monograph 107. US Department of Health and Human Services, Rockville, Maryland. pp95-212

15.   Drug Prevention: a Review of the English Language Literature Dorn, N and Murji, K (1992). ISDD, Research Monograph 5.

16.   Drug Education Programs For Young People: Reginald G Smart: A paper prepared for the "Window of Opportunity Congress", Adelaide, Australia, December 1991.

17.   Evaluation of the Effects of the Project Charlie Curriculum in Public Schools of Minnesota Ahlgren, A and Merrick S (1984). Report for Storefront/Youth Action, Rickfield, Minnesota and the University of Minnesota, Alcohol and Other Drug Abuse Programming.

18.   Curriculum Guidance: 5 Health Education
        Published by National Curriculum Council, 1990
        ISBN 1 872676 23 5 (see appendix D)

19.   Monitoring the Grant for Education Support and Training for Preventive Health Education: Summer and Autumn 1991.
        Ref: 131/92/NS A report by HMI produced by the Department for Education (DFE).

20.   Health Education in Schools: HEA Research Department
        Public Health Division report by MORI 1989

21.   Resolution of the Council and of Ministers of Education meeting within the Council of 23 November 1988 concerning health education in schools: Official Journal of the European Communities (89/C 3/01).

22.   "Our Policeman" Good Practice in Police/School Liaison
        A Survey by HM Inspectorate
        Published by Dept of Education and Science, 1989
        ISBN 0 85522 207 7

APPENDIX C

Sources for factual and educational material relevant to the prevention of drug misuse

ADFAM NATIONAL
> The national organisation for the families and friends of drug users
>
> First Floor
> Chapel House
> 18 Hatton Place
> London EC1N 8ND
> Tel: 071 405 3923

HEA
> Health Education Authority
> Hamilton House
> Mabledan Place
> London WC1H 9TX
> Tel: 071 383 3833

HEBS
> Health Education Board for Scotland
> Woodburn House
> Canaan Lane
> Edinburgh
> Tel: 031 447 8044
>
> The Health Promotion Agency for Northern Ireland
> 18 Ormeau Avenue
> Belfast BT2 8HS
> Tel: 0232 644811

HEALTHWISE Helpline Ltd
> 9 Slater Street
> Liverpool
> L1 4BW
> Tel: 051 707 2262/0800 665544 *(from Merseyside)*
>   0800 838909 *(from outside Merseyside)*
> Fax: 051 708 9984

HPAW	Health Promotion Authority for Wales
	Brunel House
	2 Fitzalan Road
	Cardiff CF2 1EB
	Tel: 0222 472472

ISDD	Institute for the Study of Drug Dependence
	1 Hatton Place
	London EC1N 8ND
	Tel: 071 430 1991

	THE MERSEY DRUG TRAINING AND INFORMATION CENTRE
	27 Hope Street
	Liverpool L1 9BQ
	Tel: 051 709 3511

NYA	The National Youth Agency Information Services
	17-23 Albion Street
	Leicester LE1 6GD
	Tel: 0533 471200

PHCS	Pharmacy Health Care Scheme
	Royal Pharmaceutical Society of Great Britain
	1 Lambeth High Street
	London SE1 7JN
	Tel: 071 735 9141

RE-SOLV	The Society for the Prevention of Solvent Abuse
	30a High Street
	Stone
	Staffordshire ST15 8AW
	Tel: 0785 817885

SCODA	Standing Conference on Drug Abuse
	1-4 Hatton Place
	London EC1 8ND
	Tel: 071 430 2341

SCOTTISH DRUGS FORUM
5 Oswald Street
Glasgow G1 4QR
Tel: 041 221 1175

TACADE   The Advisory Council on Alcohol and Drug Education
1 Hulme Place
The Crescent
Salford M5 4QA
Tel: 061 745 8925

A P P E N D I X   D

National Curriculum Council: Curriculum Guidance 5: Health Education

The drug education content of the National Curriculum Science Order for England and Wales 1991[*] was described in chapter 5.2. The four age groups, referred to as 'key stages' in the order, are also addressed in Curriculum Guidance 5: Health Education which provides detailed guidance on what each key stage could contain, as follows:

Substance use and misuse
The acquisition of knowledge, understanding and skills which enable pupils to consider the effect of substances such as tobacco, alcohol and other drugs on themselves and others and to make informed and healthy decisions about the use of such substances.

KEY STAGE 1 (age 5-7)
Substance use and misuse

- know that all medicines are drugs but not all drugs are medicines;

- know that all substances can be harmful if not used properly;

- know about different types of medicine and that some people need them to live a normal life;

- know and understand simple safety rules about medicines, tablets, solvents, household substances.

KEY STAGE 2 (age 7-11)
Substance use and misuse

- know that all medicines are drugs but not all drugs are medicines;

- know that there are over-the-counter, prescribed, legal and illegal substances and have some understanding of their effects;

- know how to make simple choices and exercise some basic techniques for resisting pressure from friends and others;

- know the important and beneficial part which drugs have played in society.

KEY STAGE 3 (age 12-14)
Substance use and misuse

- recognise personal responsibility for decisions about substance use;

- know the basic facts about substances including their effects and relevant legislation;

- be aware of myths, misconceptions and stereotypes linked with substance use;

- develop appropriate techniques for coping with situations in which substance use occurs.

KEY STAGE 4 (age 14-16)
Substance use and misuse

- explore the historical, cultural, political, social and economic factors relating to the production, distribution and use of drugs worldwide;

- understand that Britain is a drug-using society and recognise the different patterns of use and their effects, eg transmission of HIV infection through shared needles and the detrimental effect on the foetus of all types of drug use;

- recognise that individuals are responsible for choices they make about drug use;

- be able to analyse safe levels of intake; eg tobacco use is never safe, limited use of alcohol may be;

- discuss the role of the media in influencing attitudes towards drugs, particularly smoking and alcohol;

- be able to communicate effectively and confidently with those who administer medication.

The statutory Science Order referred to in section 6.2 included a timetable for the four key stages to be implemented. This was as follows:

1 August 1992
1st key stage - all pupils in that key stage

2nd key stage - pupils in the first three years of that stage

3rd key stage - all pupils in that key stage

4th key stage - pupils in the first year of that key stage

1 August 1993
2nd key stage - all other pupils

4th key stage - all other pupils

* Statutory Instruments 1991 Education, England and Wales The Education (National Curriculum) (Attainment Targets and Programmes of Study in Science) Order 1991

A P P E N D I X   E

Extract from report by the National Liaison Group of Coordinators of Health and Drugs Education in England and Wales:

Some key principles underpin the work of HECs and examples of putting them into practice will demonstrate the range of work that DECs and HECs have been involved in since 1986. These principles fall under four headings:

- *Starting where a client (young person, adult, institution) is:*
A class of five year olds bring a variety of knowledge, attitudes and skill to learning situations involving health. The experiences of adults lead to a greater variety and complexity of responses to be taken into account. Education can only effectively start at the level of knowledge and understanding that the student demonstrates or declares. This leads to:

- *The use of appropriate methodology*
In order to involve and empower people in making health related or harm minimisation decisions about their lifestyles, teaching and learning strategies need to attend to:

- consideration of attitudes and values

- provision of comprehensive, unbiased and accurate information about topics and also the availability of advice and support which is relevant and appropriate

- development of self-esteem and personal, social and situational decision making skills

The process by which learning takes place is as important as the content. Active learning techniques appear to be the most effective way of addressing these issues with young people and with adults. These techniques are most successful within the context of a holistic approach to health education which suggests two more key principles:

The health-promoting institution

In order that messages conveyed in teaching health education are not undermined, the ethos, relationships and management structures of an institution need to be considered so that they support and reinforce those messages. These will be conveyed even more successfully if the adults concerned take part in determining the principles and strategies by which it will be delivered.

The multi-agency and multi-level community context of an institution

Educational institutions do not exist in a vacuum. A wide variety of individuals and organisations have an influence on them. It is important that all concerned have a shared understanding of each other's concerns and approaches in order to offer the most appropriate service for young people.

Putting these principles into practice is a complex task, requiring a judicious mixture of reactive and pro-active work in a variety of settings and with a wide range of people. DECs and HECs have been involved with:

Working with young people

- teaching in all phases of education

- leading other formal and informal groups in the youth and community service and voluntary organisations.

Council departments and institutions

Provision of consultation, information, advice, training, support, monitoring and evaluation has been made available to teachers and other adults who work in a school. This provision has also been made available to parents, governors, youth services staff, LEA advisory and support staff which include officers, advisors, inspectors, advisory teachers, educational psychologists, education welfare officers, catering services.

Such provision has involved:

- personal and professional development, identification and dissemination of good practice, identification, generation, dissemination and management of resources;

- the development and implementation of policy and curriculum issues such as the health promoting institution; broad-based, developmental and sequential programmes; and the National Curriculum particularly the Science Orders and Curriculum Guidance 5;

- dissemination of accurate information, which includes relevant results and rigorous research which supports educators in their decision making.

As health matters are not the sole responsibility of Local Education Authorities, liaison has been necessary with elected members, and officers of Careers, Housing, Environmental Health, Leisure, Road Safety, Probation and Social Services Departments.

Health Authorities and Police
- It is apparent in all parts of the country that liaison, training and collaborative ventures have occurred between HECs and these two agencies

- Collaboration is particularly evident with health education/promotion officers, HIV/AIDS co-ordinators, school nurses, alcohol and drug counselling services and police officers responsible for school and community liaison.

- HECs are also involved in the Regional Health Authority and District Health Authority Drug and Alcohol Groups.

Other Local Groups
- A wide variety of voluntary groups seek the expertise of HECs in order to raise their awareness about specific issues and for mutual support of local initiatives.

- These groups include the Women's Institute, the Soroptimists Lions and Rotary Clubs, church groups and the full range of organisations which involve themselves with young people.

The National Scene

-   Individuals, regional groups and the NLGCHDE have liaised and worked with national organisations such as the HEA, HMI, National Curriculum Council, National Youth Bureau/Agency, TACADE, The National AIDS Trust, The Portman Group and many others.

-   Individuals and groups have contributed to national journals and other publications

-   The NLGCHDE has had, since 1987, regular meetings at the Department for Education with the Minister responsible for health education. The purpose of these meetings has been to update both sides and to address current issues.

The international situation

-   A small number of HECs have been involved in international initiatives. It has been indicated that England and Wales are at the forefront of European developments in health education.

436pwg.kl9

APPENDIX F

EXAMPLE OF A SUBSTANCE USE AND ABUSE AWARENESS PROGRAMME ADOPTED BY A SCHOOL AS PART OF THEIR PERSONAL, SOCIAL AND HEALTH EDUCATION PROGRAMME:

Aims

The study of substance use and abuse is an integral part of the Personal, Social and Health Education programme.

It aims to allow students to acquire the knowledge, understanding and skills which enable them to consider the effects of substances such as tobacco, alcohol, medicines and other drugs on themselves and others and to make informed and healthy decisions about the use of such substances.

Methodology

Substance use and abuse is taught right across the school from Year 7 to Year 13. Every student has one thirty-minute period per day of Personal, Social and Health Education. These are delivered mainly by form tutors, but with a significant input from trained specialists, particularly in the upper school. Consistency in providing a spiral curriculum is provided by the form tutor staying with his/her form as it progresses through the school. The use of a spiral curriculum is important as this constantly keeps the information on all substances up to date and thus relevant to the student. It also emphasises to the student that the consideration of substance use and abuse is not a subject in isolation to be looked at as a "tick-box" exercise and then forgotten as the study moves on to another area of information.

The approach to this area of study takes two major routes. The first is to provide factual information and knowledge about drugs. The second is to build and develop the skills that enable a young person to analyse risks and make decisions. These two factors are so intertwined and mutually supportive that neither would fully benefit the whole child without the other.

The provision of factual information about drugs begins in Year 7 with tobacco and progresses through to alcohol and the difference between legal and illegal drugs by Year 9. By Key Stage 4 in Years 10 + 11, further information is given about a range of illegal substances that may be within the experience of the student. It is important to note that continual re-emphasis is put upon tobacco and alcohol. In addition to knowledge of the effects of substances, physically and mentally, information is given to the social effects of drug taking on the individual, friendship, groupings, family life and society.

The development of personal skills underpins the whole ethos of the school and is not seen purely as a means of aiding the student to make "positive" decisions on drug-taking. Experience has shown that the raising of self-esteem, the valuing of oneself and others, and honest acknowledgement of feelings and emotions and the ability to care and co-operate with others makes the student more able to cope critically with stressful situations. The delivery process is not didactic but pupil centred and activity-based, using a variety of tested techniques, such as games, role play, small group work and discussions.

In addition to class-room based learning, the use of other agencies is seen as crucial. Regular workshops are run with the Police, the Health Authority, Christian organisations, the Samaritans and other charities. One development that has been of great benefit to the school has been the creation of a pilot scheme in conjunction with the Health Authority for peer group learning. With this scheme, four groups of Year 11 students have undergone a weekend's residential training with specialists. Upon return to school, these students have run workshops for a variety of ages, being able to address the problems of trust, confidentiality and peer group pressure.

Training is a key component of the course for staff. To this end a series of INSET sessions have been held after school for interested staff to keep them informed of recent developments in information and process. Further, a whole Staff Development Training Day was held for all staff, based on substance use and abuse, run by the County Adviser, local youth workers, the police and representatives of the Sixth form to investigate both the local and national situations. It is considered important that all staff are involved in the programme for two reasons. Firstly, the theme cannot be just compartmentalised within a PSHE course. Instead, it is seen as a cross curricular theme, able to be addressed by all subjects. Secondly, it is vital for the pastoral care of the school that all staff are able to recognise and identify substance use and abuse.

In addition, the School Nurse has been trained by the Health Authority in drug education and is a most useful auxiliary to the programme. Various staff also regularly attend training courses on a county and national level.

Conclusion

The programme is essentially one of prevention. However, this can often be complex, not straightforward. It is important to be realistic about young people exploring the world that they are growing into, and to present an honest and balanced perspective within the framework of prevention. Thus, the end result is to enable the student to think critically and make decisions, based on full factual information.

436pwg.kl9

A P P E N D I X   G

LIST OF ABBREVIATIONS USED IN THE
MAIN TEXT OF THIS REPORT
(see also appendix C for list of organisations)

ACMD	Advisory Council on the Misuse of Drugs
AIDS	Acquired Immuno-deficiency Syndrome
BA	Bachelor of Arts
BEd	Bachelor of Education
BSc	Bachelor of Science
DEC	Drug Education Coordinator
DENI	Department of Education for Northern Ireland
DES	Department of Education and Science
DFE	Department for Education
EC	European Community
ESG	Education Support Grant
GEST	Grant for Education Support and Training
GP	General Practitioner
GTC	General Training Council for Scotland
HEA	Health Education Authority
HEBS	Health Education Board for Scotland
HEC	Health Education Coordinator
HIV	Human Immuno-deficiency Virus
HMI	Her Majesty's Inspectorate of Schools
HMSO	Her Majesty's Stationery Office
INSET	In-Service Training
ITT	Initial Teacher Training
LEA	Local Education Authority

LSD   Lysergic Acid Diethylamide

MDMA   3,4-Methelenedioxymethamphetamine
MORI   Market and Opinion Research International

NCC   National Curriculum Council
NLGCHDE   National Liaison Group of Coordinators of Health and
                Drugs Education

OFSTED   Office for Standards in Education
OHMCI   Office of Her Majesty's Chief Inspector of Schools
                (Wales)

PGCE   Postgraduate Certificate in Education
PSE   Personal and Social Education
PSHE   Personal, Social and Health Education
PTA   Parent Teacher Association

SCCC   Scottish Consultative Council on the Curriculum
SOED   Scottish Office Education Department

WHO   World Health Organisation

Designed by the Home Office Design and Illustration Branch
8 March 1993

Printed in the United Kingdom for HMSO

8382217 C23 5/93